THIS DIARY BELONGS TO

____

DEAR DIARY

by PATRICIA LEE

Published by One Faith Publishing

RICHMOND, VA, PORT HURON, MICHIGAN

onefaithpublishings@gmail.com

DATE ___________

Happy Day or Sad Day ⁉

I get to choose my day. So, I choose to be happy and positive.

Don't forget that you chose your day, so don't let anyone ruin that for you.

1. How was your day?

Dear diary ______________________________

Dear diary

Dear diary

Dear diary

DATE ___________

SOMETIMES I OVERTHINK

Do you overthink, even if you're doing a good job?

Do you overthink and question if someone really loves you?

Today, I want you to look yourself in the mirror and say, I AM ENOUGH! That's it!

Everyday tell yourself "I'm Enough!" and get on with your day, your happiness, and your loved ones, because someone is depending on you, being you.

1. What were you questioning or overthinking today?

Dear diary ______________________________

Dear diary

Dear diary

Dear diary

DATE ____________

What's your dreams?

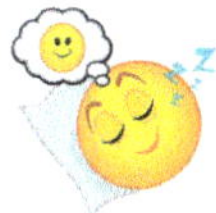

What's your dreams? Now that you have thought about it, remember what you do today will affect you and your family's future.

So, remember whether you're having a good or a bad day your choices will affect your future. Make it a good one!

1. What do you desire the most in life?

Dear diary ________________________________

Dear diary

Dear diary

Dear diary

DATE ___________

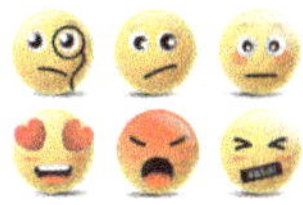

How do you feel today?

Maybe you thought everyone was staring when you walked into the class or maybe something happened that you weren't too sure of.

1. How did that make you feel?

Dear diary

Dear diary

Dear diary

Dear diary

DATE ___________

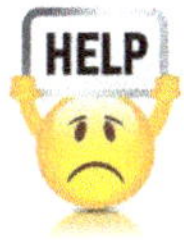

I NEED HELP!

How do you feel when you get homework that you don't understand and there is no one at home to help you understand it?

1. What do you do, and how does that make you feel?

Dear diary ____

Dear diary

Dear diary

Dear diary

DATE ___________

My very first crush!!

1. Let's talk about it.

Dear diary

Dear diary

Dear diary

Dear diary

DATE ___________

THE SCHOOL BULLY 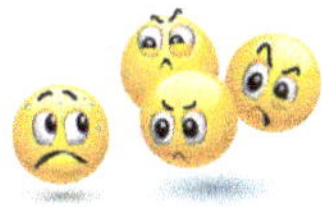

Are you or your friends being affected by the school bully?

1. How do you plan to help the situation?

Dear diary

Dear diary

Dear diary

Dear diary

DATE ___________

MY FAVORITE SUBJECT 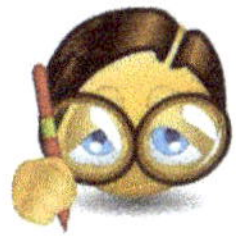

What is your favorite subject in school and my least favorite subject in school.

1. How do handle the hard stuff?

Dear diary ____

Dear diary

Dear diary

Dear diary

DATE ___________

My favorite teacher

Who's your favorite teacher?

1. I'm so happy to have this person in my life because….

Dear diary

Dear diary

Dear diary

Dear diary

DATE ___________

MY FUTURE SO BRIGHT!

The future is very close, and I really want to make sure I'm going in the right direction.

I want to be_________________________when I grow up.

Dear diary ____________________________

Dear diary

Dear diary

Dear diary

DATE ___________

WHO'S IMPORTANT TO ME?

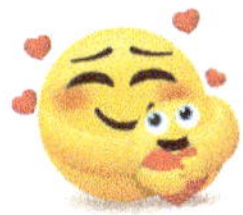

The most important person in my life is________________

1. This person is most important to me because…

Dear diary

Dear diary

Dear diary

Dear diary

DATE ___________

MY FAVORITE HOLIDAY! 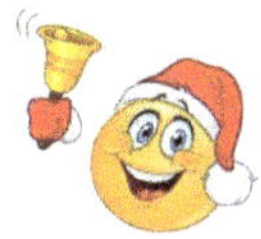

Holidays are special times, what's your favorite holidays and why?

____

1. What do holidays mean to you?

Dear diary ___________________________________

Dear diary

Dear diary

Dear diary

DATE ___________

Fun Time

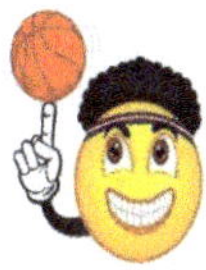

1. What things do I enjoy in school and after school that keeps me active?

Dear diary ______________________________

Dear diary

Dear diary

Dear diary

DATE ___________

LET'S DANCE!

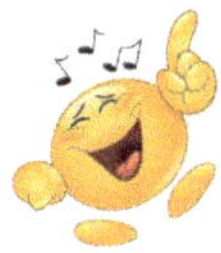

I love when we have school dances!

1. I love school dances because…

Dear diary

Dear diary

Dear diary

Dear diary

DATE ___________

TIME TO GO SHOPPING!!

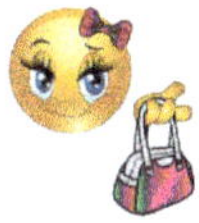

Shopping is a great way for me to have fun with my friends.

1. I love shopping because…

Dear diary ____

____

____

____

____

____

____

____

____

____

____

____

____

____

____

____

____

____

Dear diary

Dear diary

Dear diary

DATE ___________

ME & MY BESTIE! 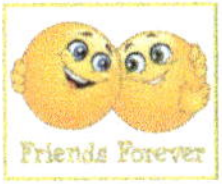

Me and my best friend.

1. What do I like the most about my best friend?

Dear diary ____

____

____

____

____

____

____

____

____

____

____

____

____

____

____

____

____

____

Dear diary

Dear diary

Dear diary

DATE ___________

IT'S OKAY TO SHARE MY FEELINGS

1. I love to communicate with my friends about things that bother me because…

Dear diary

Dear diary

Dear diary

Dear diary

DATE ____________

ZIPPER MOUTH! 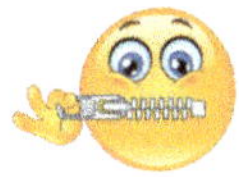

1. Sometimes communicating my problems to my parents is hard because…

Dear diary ____

Dear diary

Dear diary

Dear diary

DATE ___________

LET'S TALK!

I want to get better with telling my mom and dad things that's going on in my life.

1. Why is it important to have an open communication with my parents?

Dear diary

Dear diary

Dear diary

Dear diary

DATE ___________

PRAYING!

Praying helps me to stay connected.

1. I need to pray because...

Dear diary

Dear diary

Dear diary

Dear diary

DATE ____________

PRAYER TIME!

I love to pray, praying helps me to release a lot of things that I think that I'm not sure of.

1. What are some things that I can pray about today?

Dear diary

Dear diary

Dear diary

Dear diary

DATE ___________

MAKING A DIFFERENCE

I want to make a difference in this world, but I know it starts with me effectively making sure I absorb an education.

1. How can I make a difference in the world?

Dear diary

Dear diary

Dear diary

Dear diary

DATE ___________

Good Grades! 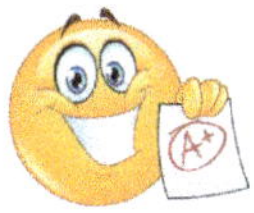

1. How do I get good grades and stay on the honor roll.

Dear diary ____

____

____

____

____

____

____

____

____

____

____

____

____

____

____

____

____

____

Dear diary

Dear diary

Dear diary

DATE ___________

MY FAVORITE PET

What's your favorite pet?

If you don't have a pet, what type of pet would you like to have?

1. How does your pet(s) make you feel?

Dear diary

Dear diary

Dear diary

Dear diary

DATE ___________

FEELING UNCOMFORTABLE

Sometimes I feel uncomfortable when people stare at me when I'm doing a new task in class.

1. I'm going to get better at blocking out distractions by…

Dear diary

Dear diary

Dear diary

Dear diary

DATE ___________

IT'S OK 2 B UNIQUE

I'm not always the most stylish one in class, and that's ok. I like to be an individual because that's what make me unique.

1. What makes me unique?

Dear diary

Dear diary

Dear diary

Dear diary

DATE ____________

Shhhhhh.... 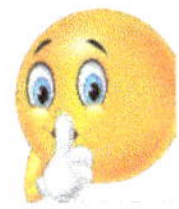

1. Quiet time for me looks like…

Dear diary ______________________________

____

____

____

____

____

____

____

____

____

____

____

____

____

____

____

____

____

____

Dear diary

Dear diary

Dear diary

DATE ___________

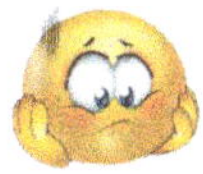

ROUGH TIMES

Everyone has rough moments.

1. What are some things that helps me to get through my rough times?

Dear diary ____

____

____

____

____

____

____

____

____

____

____

____

____

____

____

____

____

Dear diary

Dear diary

Dear diary

DATE ___________

I LOVE ME! 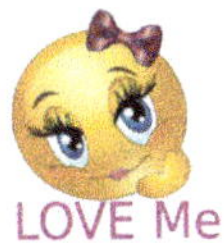

Being me is the best I can be because no one in this world can ever be me!

1. I love being me because…

Dear diary ____

____

____

____

____

____

____

____

____

____

____

____

____

____

____

____

____

Dear diary

Dear diary

Dear diary

Dear diary...

NEVER LET
ANYONE
DULL YOUR
Sparkle

DATE ___________

TODAY'S THOUGHTS...

DATE ___________

TODAY'S THOUGHTS...

DATE ____________

TODAY'S THOUGHTS...

DATE ___________

TODAY'S THOUGHTS...

Date ___________

TODAY'S THOUGHTS...

DATE ___________

TODAY'S THOUGHTS...

DATE ___________

TODAY'S THOUGHTS...

DATE ___________

TODAY'S THOUGHTS...

DATE ___________

TODAY'S THOUGHTS...

Date ___________

TODAY'S THOUGHTS...

DATE ___________

TODAY'S THOUGHTS...

DATE ___________

TODAY'S THOUGHTS...

DATE ___________

TODAY'S THOUGHTS...

DATE ___________

TODAY'S THOUGHTS...

Date ___________

TODAY'S THOUGHTS...

DATE ___________

TODAY'S THOUGHTS...

CPSIA information can be obtained
at www.ICGtesting.com
Printed in the USA
LVHW070616280323
742728LV00005B/641

9 781952 752254